JAMES MADISON'S
★ PRESIDENCY ★

Presidential Powerhouses

JAMES
MADISON'S
★ PRESIDENCY ★

ERIKA WITTEKIND

LERNER PUBLICATIONS ◆ MINNEAPOLIS

Lerner Publications Company
A division of Lerner Publishing Group, Inc.
241 First Avenue North
Minneapolis, MN 55401 USA

For reading levels and more information, look up this title at www.lernerbooks.com.

Main body text set in Caecilia LT Std 9.5/15.
Typeface provided by Adobe Systems.

Library of Congress Cataloging-in-Publication Data

Wittekind, Erika, 1980–
  James Madison's presidency / Erika Wittekind.
      pages cm — (Presidential powerhouses)
  Includes bibliographical references and index.
  ISBN 978-1-4677-7929-6 (lb : alk. paper)
  ISBN 978-1-4677-8599-0 (eb pdf)
  1. Madison, James, 1751–1836—Juvenile literature. 2. United States—Politics and government—1809–1817. 3. Presidents—United States—Biography—Juvenile literature. I. Title.
  E342.W58 2016
  973.5'1092—dc23 [B]   2015013845

Manufactured in the United States of America
1 – CG – 12/31/15

★ TABLE OF CONTENTS ★

★ INTRODUCTION ★

It took mere hours for the British to deliver one of the most crucial defeats of the War of 1812 (1812–1815). By early afternoon on August 24, 1814, British forces had overrun the inexperienced American forces at Bladensburg, Maryland, clearing a path for the British to take over the nearby US capital city. As the American lines started to collapse, President James Madison, who had accompanied his outmatched troops into battle to inspire confidence, retreated on horseback to Washington, DC.

After making sure the White House had been evacuated, Madison rode out of Washington, DC, appearing calm to onlookers despite his knowledge that the city was about to be destroyed by British troops. As nightfall descended, the hilltops along the Potomac River gave him a view of the battle's aftermath. Attorney General Richard Rush, who accompanied him, later described the devastating scene: "The columns of smoke and flame descending through the night . . . from the Capitol, the president's house, and other public edifices, as the whole were on fire, some burning slowly, others with bursts of flame and sparks rising high up in the dark horizon." But faced with this grim scene, the president refused to appear defeated. Villagers who encountered him on this journey described him as "tranquil as usual, and though much distressed by the dreadful event which had taken place, not dispirited."

A summer storm soon extinguished the flames, and word arrived that the British had departed the burned city. Madison decided the best course of action was to return as quickly as possible. This would demonstrate that while the city had fallen, the US government had not, and the president remained in power. Madison sent word to the rest of his cabinet to join him. On August 26, Madison rode the streets of Washington, DC, with Rush and his secretary of state, James Monroe. The walls of the White House were burned, blackened, and crumbling. The dome of the Capitol Building had collapsed, and the Library of Congress within it had been destroyed. The Navy Yard lay in ruin, while private residences also had been set aflame, and dead horses littered the streets.

Even in the dire surroundings, the president maintained his usual calm demeanor. As Monroe located new positions for

British troops set fire to buildings in Washington, DC, on August 24, 1814.

artillery to defend the city in case of another attack, Madison comforted the troops and residents he encountered, urging them to keep their spirits up. "Our good president is out animating and encouraging the troops and citizens, not to despair," a local banker wrote.

Not everyone shared Madison's outlook at first. While the president was visiting the Capitol, William Thornton, the architect who had designed the gutted building, delivered a message from a group of citizens who wanted to surrender to the British. After two years of fighting and the loss of their capital city, they were ready to accept defeat. But Madison forbade it, declaring that surrender was not acceptable and that no one should suggest it to the British. Thornton joined Madison's cause by rallying Washington, DC, residents to repair their city and prepare to defend it again. Likewise, the American people followed their president's lead and persevered. The United States may have lost a crucial battle in its capital city, but it had not lost the war.

James Madison is most remembered as one of the United States' founders. As a delegate at the Constitutional Convention, Madison played a major role in shaping the Constitution, the document that replaced the Articles of Confederation and established how the new country would be governed. As one of the authors of *The Federalist Papers*, he helped persuade the states to approve the new Constitution, ceding some of their power to make a stronger central government. Then, as a member of the United States Congress, he introduced and pushed for the passage of the Bill of Rights, the first ten amendments to the Constitution, which establish some of Americans' most fundamental liberties. For these reasons, Madison is often referred to as the Father of the Constitution.

While the creation and passage of these documents ranked among Madison's most historic and far-reaching accomplishments, he also went down in history as the nation's first wartime president. Standing just 5 feet 4 inches (1.6 meters) tall, the fourth president was a soft-spoken man who was often in poor health. He did not fit most people's image of a military commander, and he was reluctant to take the country to war. But he successfully led the United States through one of its first major conflicts as a new country. Through the controversial and costly War of 1812, Madison reasserted the country's independence while maintaining the constitutional rights he had fought to create.

James Madison was a short, slight man with a quiet voice.

★ CHAPTER ONE ★

SHAPING A
NEW NATION

After arriving from England in the mid-seventeenth century, James Madison's great-great grandparents made their home in the colony of Virginia. By the time James Madison Sr.—father of the future president—married Nelly Conway in 1749, the family owned a plantation called Montpelier, with thousands of acres and dozens of slaves to work it. On March 16, 1751, Nelly gave birth to James Madison Jr, called Jemmy as a child. He was the first child in what would be a large family.

Young James was plagued by illness and seizures, possibly caused by epilepsy or a similar disease. But his parents made sure his poor health did not stand in the way of an excellent education. James attended a boarding school in King and Queen County, Virginia, where he studied advanced math and learned Latin, Greek, and French. The school's extensive library served James's overflowing intellectual curiosity. He became an avid reader, writing down thoughts and questions as he read and then seeking out further reading materials to answer them. Several years later, the Madison family hired a tutor to work with all their children at home. This tutor saw great potential in James and recommended sending him to the College of New Jersey, which later became Princeton University. There, surrounded

Madison grew up on his family's plantation near Orange, Virginia. This 1818 illustration shows the main house at the Montpelier plantation.

by his intellectual peers, Madison shed some of his lifelong shyness. He became known for both his brilliance and his sense of humor, as he composed insulting poems about members of opposing debate teams. Instead of preparing himself for any particular profession, Madison studied philosophy and society. He graduated in just two years, having done well enough on his entrance exams to skip his freshman year and later completing his last two years' curriculum in a single year.

After Madison returned home to Montpelier in 1772, he took up a lifelong interest in religious freedom. The colony of Virginia's official religion was the Church of England, also called the Anglican Church, and the law did not allow the practice or spread of other religions. Madison was appalled when Virginia's government started to arrest and punish Baptist preachers for promoting their faith. Madison was an Anglican and did not approve of Baptist teachings, but he supported Baptists' right to practice their beliefs. In letters to a friend, he argued that the colony should not have an official religion at all. "Religious bondage shackles and debilitates the mind and unfits it for every noble enterprise," he wrote in 1774. His passion about religious freedom inspired him to study law. Madison believed that a diversity of ideas, in religion and politics alike, would help prevent corruption. Many competing voices would prevent one voice from becoming too powerful in society or in government.

EARLY CAREER

Before Madison could make headway on the issue of religious freedom, he became involved in a larger fight. In the 1770s, the American colonies were still under British rule. The British government had imposed several taxes on the colonists to pay debts from the French and Indian War (1754–1763). Many colonists objected to being taxed by Britain when they had no representatives in the British government. "No taxation without representation" became their rallying cry.

By 1774 colonial protests had grown louder, larger, and increasingly hostile. Madison supported resistance to British rule. Hoping to enter politics, the twenty-three-year-old started studying governance. He was especially interested in writings on limited government, religious freedom, and natural rights—freedoms he believed all people should possess. Madison also joined his county's Committee of Safety, a group that oversaw the local militia and enforced a boycott of British goods. It was Madison's first experience in public service. The militias—groups of private citizens who volunteered emergency military service—began to train. "There will by the spring, I expect, be thousands of well-trained high-spirited men ready to meet danger whenever it appears," Madison wrote of their preparation.

In the 1770s, American colonists were growing more angry about taxes they had to pay to Great Britain. Protesters in Boston threw tea into the harbor in a protest known as the Boston Tea Party.

By spring, in fact, the American Revolution (1775–1783) had broken out between colonists and British forces. As the hostilities continued, the colonies declared their independence from Britain in 1776. The same year, Madison was appointed to the Virginia Convention, the body that would draft the new state's constitution. The twenty-five-year-old Madison argued for a stronger protection of religious freedom in Virginia. His position was that religious freedom was a natural right, one that should not be limited by government. He wanted to change the wording in Article XVI from "All men should enjoy the fullest toleration in the exercise of religion" to a stronger protection, "All men are equally entitled to the free exercise of religion." Aware of his youth and inexperience, Madison did not present the amendment himself. He enlisted the help of Patrick Henry, a politician known for his skilled oratory, and Edmund Pendleton, an active member of the Church of England, who Madison hoped could win the support of other devout Anglicans. It was Madison's first foray into politics, and his talent for strategizing and picking the right allies proved successful. The amendment passed, becoming a landmark model for religious freedom.

In 1777 Madison ran for a seat in the Virginia House of Delegates. He lost the election but soon accepted a position on the Virginia Council of State, which oversaw Virginia's participation in the war. In 1779, three years after the colonies declared independence, Madison finally got his wish to participate in national politics. He was appointed as a delegate to the Second Continental Congress in Philadelphia, beginning his three-year term in 1780. Since 1775 this group of delegates representing the thirteen colonies had served as a provisional government. Its members authored the Articles of Confederation, which became the country's first constitution after the states ratified it in 1781. It formalized powers the Congress had already been exercising, such as borrowing money and creating a national navy. When the Articles were ratified, the Second Continental Congress became known as the Confederation Congress. Madison was the Congress's youngest member but quickly earned respect for his intelligence and well-researched ideas.

Charles Wilson Peale painted this portrait of Madison in 1783.

Almost as soon as the Articles of Confederation had been ratified, Madison began to argue that a stronger governmental document was needed. The Articles gave the Congress the power to regulate foreign affairs, appoint military officers, regulate currency, and borrow funds. However, it could not force states to contribute money or troops to the federal government, which hindered the war effort and gave the young country

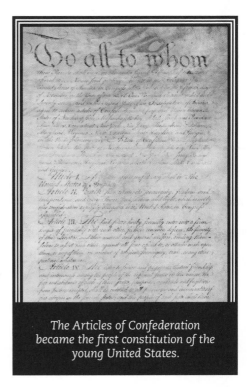

The Articles of Confederation became the first constitution of the young United States.

no way to pay off its rising debts. Madison pushed for laws that would give the Congress the power to collect and enforce federal taxes, which he thought would be necessary to achieve victory. But many of the delegates opposed Madison's ideas. They feared replacing British rule with yet another powerful government.

Madison argued that a central government that was too weak would have difficulty managing the war. Before Madison's term started, the Congress had given states the authority to raise, house, and pay the army. As soldiers went unpaid, Madison tried to secure a federal funding source. He and fellow representative Alexander Hamilton again proposed giving the federal government the power to raise and distribute funds so that it could pay its soldiers and its debts. "The idea of erecting our national independence on the ruins of public faith and national honor must be horrid to every mind which retained either

VIRGINIA HOUSE OF DELEGATES

In 1784 Madison was elected to the Virginia House of Delegates. As a member of the state legislature, he continued to push for protections of religious freedoms. He successfully lobbied for the passage of a bill that had been drafted by Thomas Jefferson in 1777 but had been tabled due to opposition from the Church of England. The bill became a model for policy debates surrounding religious rights and was later influential in Madison's drafting of the First Amendment. Madison also successfully opposed a policy proposed by Virginia's governor, Patrick Henry, which would have given state funding to Christian teachers.

honesty or pride," Madison appealed to his fellow delegates. Still, the proposal met with opposition, with one delegate, Arthur Lee, warning of the dangers of "placing the purse in the same hands as the sword." Others listened to Madison's arguments, approving an amendment that called for a 5 percent import tax and financial contributions from the states to the federal government. However, the Articles required unanimous ratification by the states, and New York rejected the amendment. By the end of the war, Madison had reached the limit of serving three one-year terms in the Continental Congress, but he would continue to lobby for a stronger government.

FATHER OF THE CONSTITUTION

After the American Revolution ended in victory for the colonists, support grew for revising the Articles of Confederation, as

Madison wanted. In a confederacy, each state holds independent power, with a relatively weak federal government connecting the states. Under the Articles of Confederation, the national government could not veto state laws or enforce national laws. But following a lengthy war, the country was faced with tremendous foreign debt. The Continental Congress had no power to raise money, and it could not force the states to tax their citizens. More people were coming around to Madison's idea of a strong central government.

In 1787 the states sent delegates to a convention to address the issue. Their job was to amend the Articles of Confederation. But Madison had a different idea. Instead of merely making changes to the Articles of Confederation, Madison proposed getting rid of the entire document and replacing it with something new. Madison's plan, called the Virginia Plan, called for a strong central government. This plan became the basic framework for the US Constitution, leading many to call Madison the Father of the Constitution. Madison's plan included three branches of government: a bicameral (two-part) legislature, an executive branch, and an independent judicial branch. In the original Virginia Plan, the states would have a proportional number of representatives to their population and the legislature would select the executive. Madison also argued for a system of checks and balances. Power would be divided among the three branches, and each branch could limit the power of the others. As Madison defended his plan, he gained a reputation for his powerful intellect and impassioned defense of his ideas. In spite of his reserved nature and quiet voice, Madison spoke more than almost any other delegate and won others over with his convincing arguments. "He always comes forward the best informed man of any point in debate," wrote fellow delegate William Pierce of Georgia.

The US Constitution divides power among three branches of government: legislative, executive, and judicial. Madison proposed this design, and it was accepted by delegates at the 1787 convention.

The delegates eventually agreed to throw out the old Articles of Confederation and make a new constitution that would strengthen the federal government, adopting Madison's three-branch design. Delegates from some smaller states worried that a legislature based strictly on population would leave their states without a real voice in the legislature, so the delegates reached a compromise. Each state would have proportional representation in the House of Representatives, with the number of representatives determined by the state's population. But every state, regardless of size, would have two senators. The delegates decided to have voters in each state vote for electors, who would then vote for the president, with the runner-up becoming the vice president. This provided a compromise between appointment by the legislature and direct election by the people, which smaller states thought would give an unfair advantage to candidates from the larger states.

The delegates did not embrace Madison's entire plan, however. Madison wanted to give the federal government the power to veto any state law. Some delegates felt it was unlikely that the states would agree to give up that much of their power. However, Madison worried that denying that power would mean the government would not be strong enough to protect individual rights. Instead, the delegates approved a clause that made US laws and treaties the "supreme law of the respective states." This became known as the supremacy clause. It meant that federal laws that conflicted with state laws would stand unless they were overturned by the court system. Madison felt this process would be too slow and would allow states to pass harmful laws before the appeals process could run its course.

George Washington (standing right) invites delegates to sign the new Constitution on September 17, 1787.

After the delegates approved the draft of the Constitution, it was sent to the thirteen states for ratification. At least nine states had to ratify the Constitution for it to become the law of the land. Delegates knew it would be a difficult task because of the way that power was being moved from the states to the federal government. Madison, along with delegates Alexander Hamilton and John Jay, wrote a series of newspaper essays supporting the Constitution. Known as *The Federalist Papers*, these essays explained the weaknesses of the Articles of Confederation and supported the new Constitution. Madison wrote twenty-nine of the eighty-five essays. He argued that the Constitution would ensure a stable republic and protect the rights of its citizens. While favoring a strong central government, he made clear that the federal government's powers still would

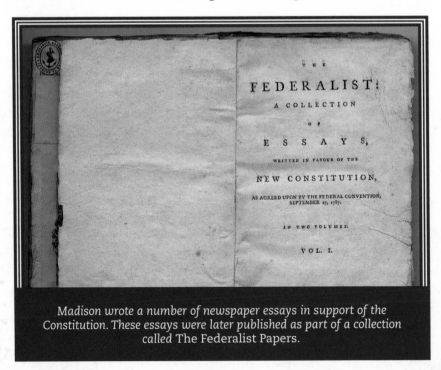

Madison wrote a number of newspaper essays in support of the Constitution. These essays were later published as part of a collection called The Federalist Papers.

CONGRESSIONAL ACCOMPLISHMENTS

Even after the ratification of the Constitution, Madison continued to play a large role in designing the US government. He was a major force in the passage of the Bill of Rights. He proposed the creation of the Departments of State, War, and Treasury as part of the executive branch, with the president having the power to appoint department heads with approval from the Senate. The president possessed sole power to remove the department heads. Madison also introduced legislation to raise money through tariffs (taxes on imported goods).

be "few and defined." By June 1788, the required nine states had ratified the Constitution, making it the official law of the land. *The Federalist Papers* remain important documents. Even in modern times, scholars use them to figure out the original meaning and intent of the words in the Constitution.

THE BILL OF RIGHTS

In 1789 Virginians elected Madison to the US House of Representatives. He beat James Monroe but remained on good terms with him, recalling later that "there was never an atom of ill will between us." Still a fervent champion of personal rights, he brought that conviction to the Capitol. One of his first actions was to sponsor a series of amendments to the Constitution that would protect individual liberties. The First Amendment, for example, protects freedom of speech, press, and other types of expression, as well as the right to religious liberty. Other amendments cover the right to bear arms, protection from unlawful search

and seizure, and other rights related to the justice system. This collection of amendments, later dubbed the Bill of Rights, was particularly important to Madison's friend and fellow politician, Thomas Jefferson. Jefferson and Madison had supported the ratification of the Constitution with the understanding that a list of protections for these human rights would soon be added to it.

Some thought the amendments were unnecessary because these rights would be recognized without being written into the Constitution. But Madison had campaigned for Congress on the promise that he would add them. He argued passionately, especially for the First Amendment rights, using the powers of persuasion for which he had become known. Largely through his efforts, the first ten amendments of the Constitution passed.

THE REPUBLICANS

At first, Madison worked tirelessly in support of President George Washington's policies. But he soon broke with the president on several issues. First, Madison opposed the proposal of Alexander Hamilton, secretary of the treasury, to create a national bank that would help the nation repay the country's debts from the American Revolution. Hamilton interpreted the Constitution to mean that Congress could pass a wide range of laws and spend public money in ways it saw fit to promote the general welfare. Madison disagreed, arguing that the Constitution limited the government's scope to powers specifically listed in the document. He thought Hamilton's ideas would lead to federal control over other areas—education, religion, law enforcement, and even roads. "In short everything from the highest object of state legislation down to the most minute object of police would be thrown under the power of Congress," Madison argued before the House.

Jefferson agreed. He and Madison joined to form the Republican Party, also called the Democrat-Republicans, to

Madison (left) and Thomas Jefferson (right) shared similar political views. Together they formed the Republican Party in 1792.

oppose the Federalists. (This party is unrelated to the modern Republican Party, which came into being much later.) According to Madison, Republicans believed that people "are capable of governing themselves."

Madison, Jefferson, and the Republicans also differed with the Federalists on foreign affairs. After France went to war against Great Britain in 1793, Washington declared the United States would be impartial. Hamilton also supported neutrality. France had been an important US ally in the American Revolution, and Madison felt that the United States was failing to live up to that friendship.

When John Adams became president in 1797, the Federalists, who controlled Congress, passed the Alien and Sedition Acts. Aimed at silencing critics of Washington's administration, these laws placed restrictions on writings and other forms of expression that opposed federal foreign policy. Those who violated the

laws were jailed. In 1797 Madison finished his term in Congress and returned home to Virginia. There he wrote the Virginia Resolution, which argued that the Alien and Sedition Acts were unconstitutional, violating the First Amendment. The Virginia state legislature passed the resolution opposing the federal law.

Madison soon returned to national politics. Jefferson became the country's third president in 1801, a victory for the Republicans. He appointed Madison secretary of state. Madison remained secretary of state for Jefferson's two terms, until 1809. When he spoke about policy decisions during those years, Madison often said, "The president has decided . . ." He declined to speak about his own policy positions so often that historians have difficulty piecing together his views from that time period. Some observers felt that Madison heavily influenced Jefferson's foreign policy decisions.

In 1803 Madison supported Jefferson on the Louisiana Purchase, land in the Mississippi River basin that the United States purchased from France. Madison also was instrumental in instituting a trade embargo on Britain and France. The two European countries had been seizing American ships as part of their own conflict. This trade ban proved unpopular and ineffective.

RUNNING FOR PRESIDENT

As his second term drew to a close, Jefferson threw his support behind Madison to be the country's next president. Republican George Clinton opposed Madison for the party's nomination. Fortunately for Madison, he had not only the president's support but that of his popular wife, Dolley, whom he had married in 1794. Dolley Madison frequently entertained congressional Republicans in the Madisons' home and persuaded many to support her husband over Clinton. The party nominated Madison for president and Clinton for vice president.

DOLLEY MADISON

In 1794 Madison was out walking when he saw Dolley Payne Todd, a widow who was seventeen years younger than him. He asked mutual friend Aaron Burr for an introduction. Already aware of Madison's accomplishments, Dolley wrote excitedly to a friend that "the great little Madison" wanted to meet her. The two were married later that year, with Dolley describing her husband on her wedding day as "the man whom of all others I most admire." Dolley's well-known love of social occasions and colorful dresses stood as a contrast to her husband's reserved personality. While the widowed Jefferson was president, she often served as hostess at the White House. After Madison was elected, she continued this role, while also advising her husband on political issues. Some historians view her as creating the role of the First Lady as an official hostess and someone with political influence of her own.

Dolley Madison advised her husband on political issues and campaigned on his behalf.

As the Republican candidate, Madison faced Federalist Charles Pinckney, who focused his campaign on the unpopularity of Jefferson's trade embargo. Pinckney's campaign even featured a cartoon mascot, a snapping turtle named Ograbme (*embargo* spelled backward). One cartoon showed the turtle taking a bite out of a merchant—suggesting that the Republican-backed embargo was only hurting American business.

Meanwhile, some took their criticism a step further, accusing Madison of trying to provoke war with Britain by catering to the French. Jefferson refuted the claim by releasing about one hundred thousand words of Madison's diplomatic correspondence with the two countries. The papers, which were read aloud in the House and Senate and published in several newspapers, showed that Madison had not been biased in his international dealings. Many thought the papers also showed how effective Madison had been as the country's secretary of state. George Tucker, an early biographer, wrote that Madison's correspondence showed his extensive knowledge, careful courtesy, and firm conviction.

Campaigning was not among Madison's many strengths. He excelled behind the scenes in politics: setting agendas, strategizing, debating ideas in committees,

Charles Pinckney, Federalist candidate for president in 1808, ran against Madison in the election.

and persuading individuals to see his point of view. But public speaking did not come naturally to him. In addition to his small size and ill health, he was known for having a weak speaking voice that was sometimes even inaudible. Most Americans knew him not through his public appearances but through his accomplishments and writings.

While Madison stayed out of the limelight, he had strong allies who campaigned on his behalf, most notably Jefferson. Despite some controversial policies, Jefferson was admired for reducing the country's debt and for maintaining peace. Still, although his party was popular, some questioned whether Madison was a true Republican. They remembered that he had worked with Federalists John Jay and Alexander Hamilton on *The Federalist Papers*. Jefferson's backing, Dolley's charm, and Madison's persuasive writings—as well as his respected record as secretary of state, congressman, and framer of the Constitution—all worked to overcome the doubt.

In late 1808, Madison won the election in a landslide, earning 122 electoral votes, compared to Pinckney's 44. Pinckney grumbled afterward, "I was beaten by Mr. and Mrs. Madison. I might have had a better chance if I had faced Mr. Madison alone." With his election, Madison would have the chance to lead the government he had helped to design.

★ CHAPTER TWO ★

CONFLICTS
WITH FRANCE
AND BRITAIN

As Madison took office in March 1809, the nation was already embroiled in an international crisis that had been brewing for years. France, under new leadership after its own revolution, had grown increasingly aggressive in Europe. It was at war with Great Britain, a conflict that had significant diplomatic and trade implications for the United States. Many Americans, including Madison, felt a loyalty to France because it had been an important ally in the American Revolution. Others thought that a good relationship and strong trade agreements with Great Britain were crucial for their young country's economic welfare. Many Americans also hoped to avoid another war against the British, which seemed increasingly likely based on recent British aggression. One of Madison's goals as he started his first term as president was avoiding war. In his inaugural address, Madison forcefully criticized both France and Great Britain. Yet he said he would still favor peaceful approaches and would go to war only as a last resort. Peace was the "true glory of the United States to cultivate," he said. Madison's reason for opposing war was a practical one. Raising

British ships fire at a French vessel during the Battle of Trafalgar on October 21, 1805. Great Britain declared war against France in 1803 in response to Napoleon Bonaparte's aggressive expansion in Europe.

an army would require the country to take on debts and tax its citizens. "War is the parent of armies; from these proceed debt and taxes; and armies and debts and taxes are the known instruments for bringing the many under the domination of the few," he had written in 1795.

MOUNTING TENSIONS

The United States' deteriorating diplomatic relations with both Great Britain and France was nothing new to President Madison. He had already been working for peace as Jefferson's secretary of state, with mixed results. It was a crisis that would dominate much of Madison's presidency.

During Jefferson's presidency, the British had started seizing American merchant ships that were headed to Europe. As the war between Britain and France dragged on, captured American sailors were forced to join Britain's Royal Navy. The practice,

During the early 1800s, when American merchant ships were captured, their sailors were often forced into the British Royal Navy.

called impressment, had become an official policy of the British government. Diplomatic missions revealed that Britain viewed US democracy as weaker than the British monarchy and that Britain did not expect the Americans to be able to stand up to the British on the impressment issue.

Meanwhile, the United States was being pressured to choose sides between two of its most significant European trade partners, France and Britain. In 1806 Jefferson and Madison had received word from France that British ships would no longer be allowed in French ports. Additionally, any merchant ships that had traded with the British—including American ships—would be barred. The British began to pressure the United States to go against France's new trade rules. But this would risk war with France, a former ally. The United States' relationship with both countries was deteriorating.

In June 1807, the US warship *Chesapeake* encountered a British ship, the *Leopard*, off the coast of Virginia. When the crew of the *Chesapeake* refused to have their ship boarded and searched, the *Leopard* fired at the American ship and then its crew boarded by force. Three Americans were killed, three taken into custody, and eighteen more injured. The attack angered many Americans. In their eyes, Britain was treating the United States like a colony instead of a sovereign nation. As secretary of state, Madison described the incident as "lawless and bloody." He sent a diplomatic message to the British, demanding that the British return the Americans who had been taken into custody, provide reparations, and end the practice of impressment. By December 1807, the British had responded that not only would they continue seizing American merchant ships and warships,

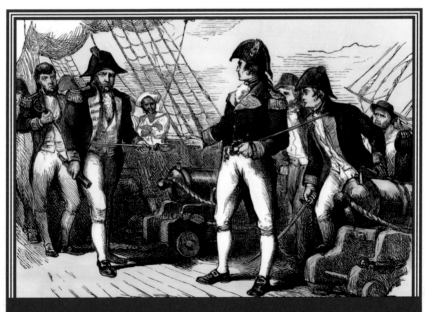

Captain James Barron (center left) surrenders the USS Chesapeake *to the British in June 1807.*

but they would step up the practice. Any ships that traded with France or with France's allies or colonies would be seized. In turn, the French warned that they would seize American ships that traded or interacted with the British.

The United States was still reluctant to go to war with these two great powers. Instead, Jefferson urged Congress to pass an embargo, ending all US trade with foreign countries. Madison wrote a series of editorials explaining the reasons for the embargo. American ships would stay safe at home, while both Britain and France would lose access to American goods and chances to sell their own goods on the US market. It would be in France's and Britain's best interest to change their methods so that trade could begin again. The fact that the embargo applied to trade with all countries made it impartial, Madison contended. Therefore, he did not think it would lead to war. Yet the damage to the US economy was tremendous. American exports dropped from $108 million in 1807 to $22 million in 1808. Unemployment was skyrocketing, and opposition to the embargo mounted.

The economic hardship caused some states to challenge federal authority. In Massachusetts the legislature outlawed enforcement of the federal embargo. The Connecticut governor refused to allow local militia to enforce the embargo. Some New Englanders even called for their states to secede from the union. Republicans in Congress responded to their constituents' rage. Shortly before Madison took office, Congress ended the embargo against Jefferson's and Madison's wishes.

ATTEMPTS AT PEACEFUL SOLUTIONS

Despite the failure of the embargo, Madison still believed that economic pressure was the best way to address the issue and that an embargo would work if left in effect for a longer period.

As a lame duck president, finishing out his term before his successor took office, Jefferson declined to take any action, so Madison took the issue upon himself in the days leading up to his inauguration. The president-elect spent February working with Virginia congressman Wilson Cary Nicholas on a more streamlined embargo. Congress passed Madison's law, called the Non-Intercourse Act. The new law still banned trade with Britain and France but lifted the embargo on trade with all other countries. If either France or Britain changed its policy on impressment, the law gave the president the power to lift the embargo for that country.

This 1807 British cartoon criticizes the American embargo. Jefferson and Madison follow orders from French emperor Napoleon Bonaparte (upper left) while Congress debates the problem (upper right). Meanwhile, the US economy suffers (lower right).

Confident in his plan to pursue peaceful solutions, Madison staffed key cabinet positions mostly with Republicans who had been loyal supporters, instead of with men who had the expertise they would need in the event of war. As his secretary of war, he chose William Eustis, a physician who had treated soldiers during the American Revolution but had no military experience beyond the infirmary. Madison selected Paul Hamilton to be secretary of the navy, a department that Madison did not think would ever be needed. Hamilton had once been a governor of South Carolina but had become known for his tendency to drink heavily during the workday.

For the position of secretary of state, Madison wanted Jefferson's secretary of the treasury, Albert Gallatin, but Gallatin was unpopular with some Republicans and could not be confirmed by the Senate. Instead, Madison kept Gallatin on in his prior position, for which he did not need to be reconfirmed. He then appointed Robert Smith, a former secretary of the navy, as his secretary of state. Because he did not fully trust Smith, Madison conducted important diplomatic communications personally.

Robert Smith served as secretary of state in Madison's cabinet.

Within months of Madison's taking office, it seemed his peaceful approach of applying economic pressure had worked. David Erskine, a representative from Britain, said his country would end its objectionable policies if the United States would resume trade. On April 19, 1809, Madison issued a proclamation that trade between the two countries would resume in June. When June came, however, he received word that the British would not uphold the agreement negotiated by its own minister. Erskine had not followed British instructions to give the United States a list of requirements. These included permission for the Royal Navy to seize American ships that were trading with the French. But the president felt the Americans could not allow this breach on their sovereignty. With Congress out of session, Madison proclaimed that trade with Britain would be halted again.

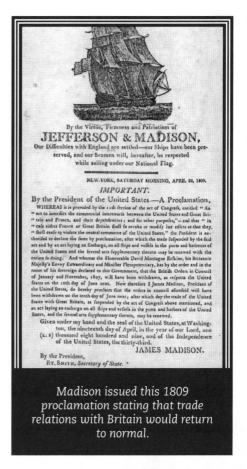

Madison issued this 1809 proclamation stating that trade relations with Britain would return to normal.

Meanwhile, Madison began to prepare for the possibility of war with Britain. He asked Congress to authorize a national militia of one hundred thousand men and to approve funds for repairing ships in the US Navy. Unsure whether the expense of a military was warranted, Congress chose not to act.

WEDNESDAY DRAWING ROOMS

In the first year of Madison's presidency, Dolley Madison began the tradition of Wednesday drawing rooms. During these social events, anyone who knew the president and his wife could join them at their residence. A military band provided entertainment while guests enjoyed coffee, fruit, and other treats. The events were known for bringing together members of opposing political parties and helping them to set aside their differences and to work together.

In 1810 Congress tried a different approach by passing Macon's Bill No. 2. The law lifted all trade restrictions, including those on France and Britain. Its goal was to encourage either France or Britain—or both—to change trade practices to be more favorable to the United States. The United States promised that if either country altered its trade practices, the United States would impose trade sanctions on the other country, unless it also changed its policies within three months. Madison supported this measure, predicting that France would take advantage of the opportunity to restore trade. Two months later, France complied. Britain, on the other hand, stated it would continue to seize all American ships unless France agreed to open trade with Britain as well.

Madison's secretary of state, Robert Smith, felt slighted by Madison's habit of conducting foreign affairs without consulting him, and he undermined the president in his diplomatic dealings. Smith communicated to British leaders that he did not think France had upheld its promise to the United States to lift

James Monroe (above) became secretary of state following the dismissal of Robert Smith in 1811.

trade restrictions between the two, making Britain even less likely to change its own policies. Madison responded by removing Smith from his post, replacing him with James Monroe in 1811.

Congress followed through on the threat contained in Macon's Bill No. 2 and reinstated the embargo on trade with Britain. Madison supported the measure, with little choice but to bring the country one step closer to war with Britain.

MOVING TOWARD WAR

Meanwhile, British ships had started a blockade outside New York Harbor. They seized ships headed to France or elsewhere and forced American sailors to serve in the Royal Navy. The British were also looking for British seaman who had deserted the navy by joining American ships. As the United States tried to defend its trade routes, the USS *President* exchanged cannon fire with a British warship. The British claimed the Americans fired first, and they sent a new minister to the United States to threaten retaliation. The minister restated the British position that France would have to resume trade with Britain before Britain would stop impressment of American ships and sailors. The French also had begun to seize American ships again. But because the United States had never been under French rule, its main conflict was

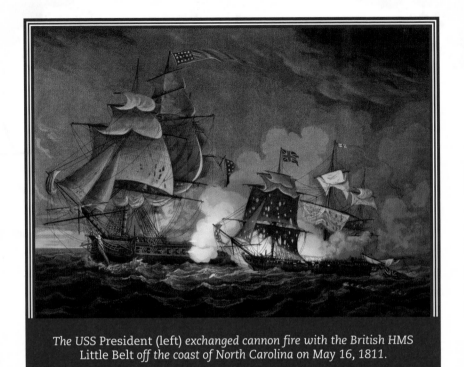

The USS President *(left) exchanged cannon fire with the British HMS* Little Belt *off the coast of North Carolina on May 16, 1811.*

with Britain and what many Americans perceived as a threat to their independence. None of the peaceful tactics the United States had tried had worked. Madison felt increasingly certain that war was the only option left.

As members of a newly elected Congress took their seats in November 1811, Speaker of the House Henry Clay expressed his support for going to war to fight for the country's continued independence from Britain. Many other new House members also felt that the United States could no longer tolerate the insulting behavior from Britain. They felt Britain was still treating the United States as if it were under British rule instead of an independent nation. Standing before the new Congress, Madison called British aggression an act of war. He urged Congress to prepare for war and to raise an army. "With this evidence of hostile inflexibility in trampling on rights which no independent nation can relinquish, Congress will feel the duty of putting the United States into an armor and an attitude demanded by the crisis," Madison said in his address.

Congress approved a volunteer army of twenty-five thousand men for five years. This was more troops than Madison had requested and a number he felt would be difficult to raise or pay for. So in March 1812, Congress approved a series of taxes that would be collected if the country went to war.

CHAPTER THREE

GOING TO WAR

The president knew that a conflict with Britain would be fought based on the powers laid out in the Constitution. According to the Constitution, only Congress has the power to declare war. The president is in charge of actually conducting the war. Heeding the Constitution, Madison hesitated to get too involved in Congress's decision. However, Congress was reluctant to declare the war without some decisive action by the president.

In January 1812, a man calling himself Count Edward de Crillon approached government officials with an intriguing offer. The man claimed to have letters from a spy who had been hired by the Canadian government to investigate the New England states' willingness to rejoin the British Empire. Madison's advisers thought that, if true, this news showed that Britain was maneuvering to take control of New England. Such a development would anger Americans and possibly help to spur Congress into action. Madison used $50,000 from the State Department budget to purchase the letters. The letters turned out to contain only vague insinuations and propaganda. Having been unsuccessful in his original mission, the spy had partnered with the man who posed as a count to sell the letters to the Americans. The spy's claims were empty, yet the brief anger they

inspired moved Congress closer to taking action. In preparation, Madison asked for and received another embargo against the British in March 1812. The new embargo would be in effect until July 4. This time, the point of the embargo wasn't to prevent war, but rather to prepare for it by bringing American ships home.

Encouraged by the support for the new embargo, Madison asked Congress to declare war on June 1. He listed his reasons before the joint session: the impressment of American sailors into the Royal Navy, the blockades that prevented American ships from safely leaving or arriving in harbors at home and abroad, and the confiscation of American ships on neutral seas. He also accused the British of encouraging hostilities from American Indians. While this charge may have held some truth, most

BY THE PRESIDENT
OF THE
United States of America,
A PROCLAMATION:

WHEREAS the Congress of the United States, by virtue of the Constituted Authority vested in them, have declared by their act, bearing date the eighteenth day of the present month, that WAR exists between the United Kingdom of Great Britain and Ireland, and the dependencies thereof, and the United States of America and their territories; Now, therefore, I, JAMES MADISON, President of the United States of America, do hereby proclaim the same to all whom it may concern: and I do specially enjoin on all persons holding offices, civil or military, under the authority of the United States, that they be vigilant and zealous, in discharging the duties respectively incident thereto: And I do moreover exhort all the good people of the United States, as they love their country; as they value the precious heritage derived from the virtue and valor of their fathers; as they feel the wrongs which have forced on them the last resort of injured nations; and as they consult the best means, under the blessing of Divine Providence, of abridging its calamities; that they exert themselves in preserving order, in promoting concord, in maintaining the authority and the efficacy of the laws, and in supporting and invigorating all the measures which may be adopted by the Constituted Authorities, for obtaining a speedy, a just, and an honorable peace.

IN TESTIMONY WHEREOF I have hereunto set my hand, and caused the seal of the United States to be affixed to these presents.

(SEAL.)

DONE at the City of Washington, the nineteenth day of June, one thousand eight hundred and twelve, and of the Independence of the United States the thirty-sixth.
(Signed)   JAMES MADISON.

By the President,
(Signed)   JAMES MONROE, Secretary of State.

After days of secret debate, Congress approved the president's request to declare war. A proclamation of the details was issued on June 19, 1812.

American Indian nations were fighting to prevent US expansion into their lands, not to aid the British. Regardless, Madison used the argument because it was persuasive. On June 4, the House voted to declare war. The Senate debated in secret for two weeks before finally approving the measure. The votes were cast along party lines—with almost all Republicans in support and all Federalists opposed.

FIGHT FOR CANADA

Having lost its trading partners in the United States and much of Europe, Britain had begun to rely on Canada as an important source of supplies. Madison thought the United States could apply more pressure to Britain by cutting off British access to Canadian goods. Although Canada was part of the British Empire, US leaders believed Britain had left this land largely undefended while at war in Europe. Additionally, many Canadians were of French descent and were thought to have little loyalty to Britain. Madison and his advisers expected many Canadians to welcome an American invasion.

The president decided to take advantage of Britain's perceived weakness in Canada. He would send US troops to attack Canada before the British had a chance to send reinforcements from overseas. He expected to use control of Canadian territory to negotiate for better trade policies, leading to a quick end to the conflict. He thought this plan would put the British at a disadvantage and still avoid a full-scale war with Britain. And he hoped to achieve some control of Canada by the time he ran for reelection in the fall of 1812.

Madison instructed his secretary of war, William Eustis, to send scouts to Canada to report on British defenses there. The scouts' reports confirmed the Republicans' optimism that fighting in Canada would be quick and successful. Eustis divided

the army into a western and eastern invasion, with the idea that the British in Canada would have to divide its own forces. But it turned out that the Americans had underestimated the British military presence in Canada. The American army, which then numbered approximately twelve thousand troops, was ill-prepared to fight a war. It was disorganized, lacked consistent supply lines, and often ran out of money. The generals

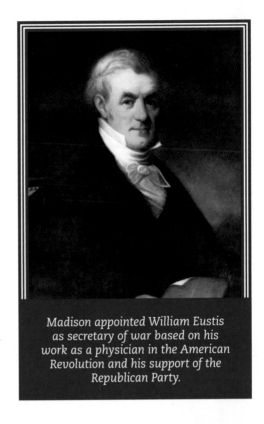

Madison appointed William Eustis as secretary of war based on his work as a physician in the American Revolution and his support of the Republican Party.

put in charge of invading Canada did not communicate with each other or with Eustis. Beneath them, state militia leaders squabbled with federal army commanders for control. Madison's hopes for a swift victory were dashed.

MILITARY DISARRAY

In Michigan, Madison put William Hull, a veteran of the American Revolution, in charge of two thousand troops based in Detroit, with instructions to invade Canada from there. Hull told Madison he did not have enough troops to fight a war, but soon Madison ordered Hull to attack Fort Malden, just across the Canadian border. Though Hull attempted to carry out his orders, his troops were poorly trained, and tensions erupted between his officers and state militia leaders. Meanwhile, the British had learned

of the Americans' plans. They rallied Canadians—who were not as eager to be liberated from British rule as Americans had believed—to defend Fort Malden. Canadians and their American Indian allies drove Hull's men back across the American border and then moved south to lay siege to Detroit. After getting word that a large army of Canadian and American Indian reinforcements was approaching Detroit, Hull surrendered Detroit on August 16.

Madison planned to send Monroe, his secretary of state, to lead troops in reclaiming Michigan. But before he could, Indiana governor William Henry Harrison, acting on his own, took command of local militia. Harrison had previously refused to work under Monroe, and instead of challenging the Indiana governor, Madison put him in charge of the federal forces in the Northwest Territory. However, Harrison's troops encountered American Indian resistance along the way and never even reached Detroit.

In the East, several New England governors refused to call up the state militia to fight in the war, in violation of federal law. Madison chose not to anger these states by enforcing the law and relied instead on militia from other states,

William Hull (right) surrenders Detroit to the Canadian army and their American Indian allies on August 16, 1812.

along with the federal army. Madison selected General Henry Dearborn as commander in the East. Dearborn mustered troops in Boston but didn't provide leadership to troops that were mustering in three other cities. To buy time to get organized, Dearborn negotiated a temporary cease-fire with the province of Lower Canada on August 8. The British took this to mean that the Americans had surrendered completely. Once word of the cease-fire and Britain's interpretation reached Madison, the president ordered Dearborn to invade eastern Canada. But by then, confused militia troops had started to return home. For those that remained to fight, confusion and distrust abounded between the state-run militia and the federal army. A militia leader working under Dearborn in New York tried to prove his loyalty by invading the Niagara Peninsula, a strip of land between Lake Ontario and Lake Erie. But some of his men refused to go with

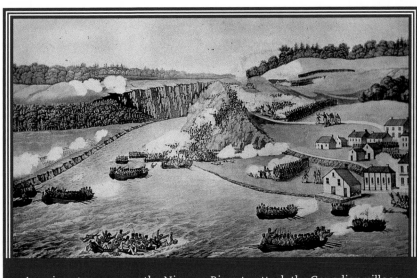

American troops cross the Niagara River to attack the Canadian village of Queenston, Ontario, on October 13, 1812. British forces drove the Americans back across the river.

him, and those who did were taken prisoner. Dearborn finally tried to set up camp across the Canadian border in November. But in their confusion, federal troops mistakenly fired on the state militia. In disarray, the Americans retreated.

The US Navy had better luck. Unlike the land forces, which were led by aging commanders from the American Revolution, the country's naval commanders tended to be youthful, well trained, and itching to prove themselves. One of these was Isaac Hull, who commanded the USS *Constitution*. On August 19, 1812, about 750 miles (1,200 kilometers) off the East Coast, the USS *Constitution* encountered the British warship HMS *Guerriere*. After an exchange of cannon fire, the *Guerriere* surrendered, giving the US forces a much-needed victory. The American ship's ability to withstand cannon fire earned it the nickname Old Ironsides.

The USS Constitution *(left) defeats the HMS* Guerriere *in a victory for the US Navy on August 19, 1812.*

NAVAL POWER

Before the war, Republicans had opposed the building of naval forces, and Madison had wavered on the issue. During the Continental Congress, he supported a small peacetime navy. By the 1790s, he had changed his mind, thinking the presence of a navy might provoke war with Britain. As the War of 1812 started, the US Navy had 7 frigates (small warships), compared to 245 in the Royal Navy. Of the 7 US frigates, 6 had been constructed during George Washington's presidency, two decades earlier. The British also had 191 larger warships with more guns. The United States had no ships of that size. In spite of these differences, the Royal Navy was undermanned, padded with inexperienced and foreign sailors, while the Americans manned their small number of ships with experienced, well-trained crews. As a wartime president, Madison quickly was convinced of the navy's usefulness and supported its expansion.

This famous naval victory did not do anything concrete to turn the tide of the war, but it boosted American morale at a time when the conflict had started to seem foolhardy and unwinnable. It was just what Madison needed as he sought to convince the United States to give his policies a chance to work through a second presidential term.

CHAPTER FOUR

WAR IN MADISON'S SECOND TERM

As the war dragged on, with few American victories, Madison's popularity dipped. In the 1812 presidential election, Madison faced a new opponent from within his own party. His vice president, George Clinton, had died earlier that year. But George Clinton's nephew, DeWitt Clinton, stepped in to oppose Madison in the election. Clinton tried to win support from both Federalists and Republicans. In the northern states, where the war was most unpopular, Clinton campaigned on the promise of peace. In the South, he promised more effective leadership of a continued war effort. Due to the slow pace of long-distance communication, many people never realized he was arguing both sides of the issue. Clinton won the support of many Federalists this way, as well as a portion of antiwar Republicans. Yet Clinton was a relative newcomer and lacked Madison's political clout. That, along with several key US naval victories and a growing desire for revenge against the British, was enough to push Madison

over the top in a tightly contested election. Madison, running on a ticket with pro-war Federalist Elbridge Gerry, won with 128 electoral votes, compared to Clinton's 89. The vote was so close in Pennsylvania that it took a month to recount. If Pennsylvania's 25 electoral votes had gone to Clinton, Madison would have lost.

DeWitt Clinton opposed Madison in the 1812 presidential election. Madison narrowly beat Clinton in the race.

GREATER STRENGTH, GROWING DIVISION

In the lead-up to the 1812 election, Madison continued to press for an expansion of the US Navy. As he awaited the election results, Madison and the First Lady attended a party aboard the USS *Constellation*, to shore up national support for the successful navy. The congressional members who attended the party would vote days later on Madison's proposal to expand the fleet, which Congress readily approved.

Before the end of 1812, Madison asked Congress to bring militias under federal control, which would have eased the persistent leadership squabbles between federal and militia leaders that were hindering the war effort. But Congress voted against this last request, citing a reluctance to take control away from the states. Next, Madison tried to shore up leadership problems in the military and within his cabinet. Madison asked James Monroe to replace William Eustis as secretary of war. Monroe declined. He planned to run for president in 1816, and he thought overseeing the war would hurt his chances. Because Federalists opposed the war and the Republicans were divided on it, Madison was left with few choices for the job. Finally, he settled on John Armstrong, a Republican with military experience, even though neither Madison nor Monroe trusted his loyalty to the administration. Meanwhile, Paul Hamilton was replaced with William Jones, a sea captain and former congressman, as secretary of the navy.

The generals who had lost so badly early in the war were widely criticized. But some Americans blamed these failures on the president. Henry Clay, who had been Madison's ally in convincing Congress to declare war, had doubts about the president's handling of the conflict. He said that Madison's mild personality was more suited to times of peace and that he was not fit for the tougher decisions of military conflict. But Clay had praise for the president in another respect. Clay recalled that years before, the Federalists had tried to silence their opposition with the Alien and Sedition Acts. Although Madison currently faced strong criticism, and his war was controversial, he did nothing to silence his critics. Even when members of his own party pressured him to support a

Henry Clay argued in favor of the declaration of war. After a series of setbacks, Clay began to doubt that Madison's mild personality was suited for the role of commander in chief.

sedition law for the duration of the war, Madison refused. Instead, the president had upheld Americans' First Amendment rights to free speech and freedom of the press.

HOPE AND SETBACKS

Early in 1813, US forces finally started making gains. The US Navy continued to fare well on the seas. On land, American troops achieved an important victory, capturing York, which is part of present-day Toronto, Canada. "The attack and capture of York is the presage of future and greater victories," Madison assured Congress when it reconvened in May 1813. But American losses in the battle were high, and the British were angry about the burning of government buildings in York.

During the attack on York, British troops blew up their gunpowder supply and destroyed their fort. The explosion caused heavy casualties to the American troops nearby, including the death of General Zebulon Pike (above).

The United States also had new money problems. Without a national bank, the US government had no central source of funds. Federalists, who supported the bank but opposed the war, persuaded many private banks not to loan the federal government money. To fund the war, Madison had to ask Congress to raise taxes, even though the Republicans usually opposed taxes.

By then Madison was anxious to end the costly and unpopular war. This priority became more urgent when Russia, an ally of Britain, dealt France a major defeat in Europe. With their French opponents weakened, the British would be able to focus more effort on defeating the Americans. At this time, Russian czar Alexander I offered to negotiate between the United States and Britain. Though Russia was a British ally, the nation hoped to resume trade with the United States if the conflict could be resolved. Eager to get the United States out of the war, Madison hoped Russia would persuade Britain to participate in negotiations. Even before Britain agreed, the hopeful president selected three delegates to send to Russia for peace talks. To achieve peace, Madison was prepared to offer to turn over British seamen who tried to join American ship crews. This would eliminate one of Britain's reasons for seizing American ships. But Britain had such an advantage in the war by then that the British refused to send negotiators.

In June the president fell ill with a fever, chills, and vomiting. He was confined to bed for three weeks, while his political enemies spread rumors about his health. Some said that Madison was unlikely to live for more than a few months. Others claimed the illness had affected the president's mind. The sick president heard reports of several more land defeats and ordered General Dearborn's removal as commander in the East. While the president was still recovering, Britain went on the attack. A fleet of British naval ships arrived on American shores and burned coastal cities.

Oliver Hazard Perry (standing) abandons the damaged USS Lawrence during the Battle of Lake Erie on September 10, 1813. He rowed to the USS Niagara where he resumed command of the fleet and defeated the British.

When Madison was feeling well enough, he and Dolley went to Montpelier, where he liked to spend part of each year. Resting at home, he decided that the Americans needed to take control of Lake Erie and Lake Ontario to secure the Canadian border. He sent Master Commandant Oliver Hazard Perry to achieve this. Word that Perry had succeeded in securing Lake Erie arrived by late September. "We have met the enemy and they are ours," Perry wrote.

Lake Erie was important because it served as a major supply route to the British army. With their supplies cut off, British soldiers in Michigan withdrew into Canada, finally relinquishing Detroit. Led by General William Henry Harrison, the Americans pursued them and won a victory at the Battle of the Thames, near the Thames River in the area of present-day southern Ontario.

Shawnee Indians fought alongside British troops in the Battle of the Thames on October 5, 1813. During the battle, Chief Tecumseh was killed by American gunfire.

By then most of the US coast faced a British blockade, except for New England. Federalists in New England, where the war was most unpopular, had defiantly continued to trade with European merchants, against the president's wishes. Madison quietly campaigned for Congress to pass another embargo, barring all American exports and British imports. He knew this would anger residents of the New England states. But Madison did not want any American-made goods helping the British fight against the United States in the war. Congress had refused to pass an embargo earlier in the year, but as the war wore on, more lawmakers agreed with the president. This embargo was short-lived, though. Britain soon defeated France and resumed trade with most of Europe. Britain no longer needed American supplies, so the embargo had no effect except to harm the American economy. Madison asked Congress to reverse its position, and Congress repealed the policy. Some used this as a basis to

criticize the president for being inconsistent. Congressman John Calhoun came to the president's defense. Although he had not supported Madison's embargo policy, he praised the president for being flexible when the circumstances changed. "Men cannot always go straightforward, but must regard the obstacles which impede their course," Calhoun said.

Meanwhile, the British had several more victories. They captured Fort Niagara and extended their blockade into New England. As Madison had feared, their success in Europe also put them in a position to send more troops to the United States. Under new leadership, the US military had grown much more effective. But no one thought American troops could withstand a full-scale British invasion. Madison worried that Washington, DC, would be a target.

US civilians help soldiers defend Fort Niagara during a suprise attack on the evening of December 18, 1813. British troops captured the fort and remained in control of the outpost until the end of the war.

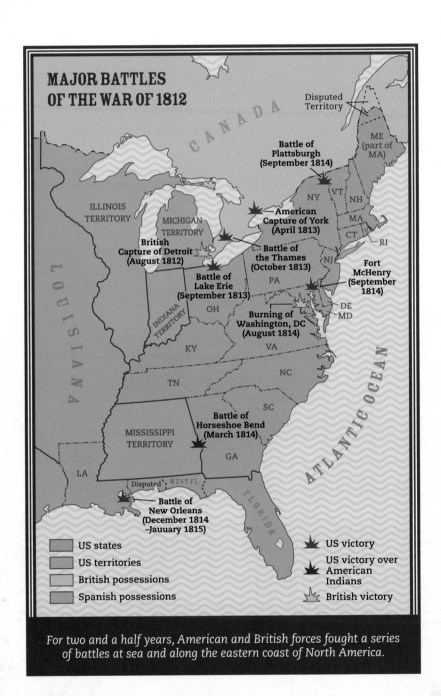

MAJOR BATTLES OF THE WAR OF 1812

CANADA

Disputed Territory

Battle of Plattsburgh (September 1814)

ME (part of MA)

ILLINOIS TERRITORY

MICHIGAN TERRITORY

American Capture of York (April 1813)

NY VT NH

MA

CT

RI

British Capture of Detroit (August 1812)

Battle of the Thames (October 1813)

NJ

Fort McHenry (September 1814)

Battle of Lake Erie (September 1813)

LOUISIANA

PA

OH

DE MD

INDIANA TERRITORY

Burning of Washington, DC (August 1814)

KY

VA

TN

NC

MISSISSIPPI TERRITORY

Battle of Horseshoe Bend (March 1814)

SC

GA

LA

Disputed WEST FL

ATLANTIC OCEAN

FLORIDA

Battle of New Orleans (December 1814 –Jauuary 1815)

US states

US territories

British possessions

Spanish possessions

US victory

US victory over American Indians

British victory

For two and a half years, American and British forces fought a series of battles at sea and along the eastern coast of North America.

Britain, seeing the improvement in American forces, was finally ready to negotiate an end to the war. Madison eagerly sent his representatives to meet with British delegates in Ghent, Belgium. But they soon reported that Britain was unwilling to stop impressment. Instead, Britain was making even more demands on the United States. The British wanted to restrict US trade and take control of the Great Lakes. On June 27, 1814, the president met with his cabinet. They decided to give up on the issue of impressment. With the war over in Europe, Britain would no longer have a need for US ships and sailors, so it was unlikely to remain a problem. The president instructed his representatives in Europe to negotiate a treaty that did not address impressment, hoping that this would be enough for Britain to give up on its other demands.

DEFENDING THE CAPITAL

While waiting for the results of the peace negotiations, Madison took action to protect the capital. He ordered a military force of more than three thousand troops, along with ten thousand militiamen, to be ready to defend Washington, DC, as well as the nearby Maryland cities of Baltimore and Annapolis. But the secretary of war, John Armstrong, failed to act quickly enough to raise the large number of troops needed. While citizens of Washington, DC, became increasingly convinced that they would be attacked, Armstrong thought the attack would be on Baltimore. Monroe disagreed. He accompanied a group of scouts and saw the British landing at Benedict, Maryland, about 34 miles (54 km) from the capital. The next day, Monroe told the president the British seemed to be planning a surprise attack on the capital.

Madison had put Brigadier General William Winder in command of the army that was charged with protecting the capital. Madison believed that Winder, the nephew of Maryland governor Levin Winder, would have the clout to gain the governor's cooperation

in raising enough troops to defend the capital. Governor Winder assured his nephew that he would send the three thousand men Madison had requested. But after fewer than three hundred enlisted soldiers reported for duty, the general had to issue an emergency call for area militiamen to join them. By August 22, 1814, he had about eighteen hundred troops, a fraction of the military force Madison had ordered. Nearby, US commodore Joshua Barney

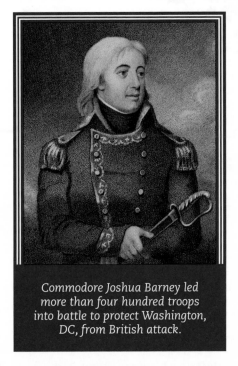

Commodore Joshua Barney led more than four hundred troops into battle to protect Washington, DC, from British attack.

was fleeing the British with his fleet of ships on the Patuxent River. Instead of letting his ships be captured, Barney decided to blow them up. He and his four hundred men then joined with Winder's troops. They marched toward the British forces, believed to number from five thousand to seven thousand.

Later that evening, the president joined his forces, hoping his presence would inspire them to confidence. Madison left Dolley at the White House with instructions to protect herself and the nation's important papers. The First Lady and a few servants loaded documents into wagons to be hidden. The next day, Madison wrote to her that the troops "were in high spirits and make a good appearance." But most of them had only recently left their homes. They lacked training and organization. Some of them had only muskets instead of long-range rifles, because Armstrong was keeping the available rifles for the troops fighting in the North.

SAVING WASHINGTON'S PORTRAIT

As one of her last acts before fleeing Washington, DC, Dolley Madison ordered two staff members to break the frame of a portrait of George Washington so that the canvas could be removed and transported out of the White House. She did not want the British to humiliate the Americans by destroying the portrait of the country's first president. At her urging, a pair of unidentified New Yorkers brought the painting first to a mill and later to a Virginia farmhouse for safekeeping. Unknown to the First Lady, the portrait she saved was a copy, not the original painting.

Dolley Madison (left) and White House servants moved important documents, books, and artifacts, including a portrait of George Washington (right), into hiding to protect them from the advancing British troops.

FACING DEFEAT

On August 23, the British troops attacked Washington, DC. As Madison's fears were confirmed, he wrote again to Dolley, warning her to be prepared to leave. Overnight, Madison learned that seven hundred more US troops had arrived from Virginia but needed weapons. Then the president received word that Winder, fearing an overnight attack, had retreated back to the capital. His twenty-five hundred troops had encamped near the Potomac River, where they thought the British would approach. Another two thousand militiamen, responding to Winder's urgent call for militia, gathered at a bridge near Bladensburg, Maryland. At midnight Madison received word that the British had begun marching toward Washington, DC.

Early the following morning, Madison joined his general and several cabinet members, including Monroe, William Jones, Richard Rush, and later Armstrong. Then they learned the British would arrive at the capital through Bladensburg. Concerned about Armstrong's questionable leadership and wanting to give his ill-prepared troops a confidence boost, Madison marched with Winder's men to meet the British. In doing so, he became the last US president to lead troops into combat while in office. As the battle began, the president and his top advisers moved to the rear of the troops for protection. At first, the British fell back under the attack of American artillery fire. But they soon pressed forward again and overwhelmed the American forces. The battle lost, the president quickly retreated toward the city.

Madison knew what was coming, so he sent a warning ahead. A messenger arrived at the White House, calling for Dolley Madison to "Clear out! Clear out!" Dolley was reluctant to leave, writing to her sister, "I am determined not to go myself until I see Mr. Madison safe, so that he can accompany me," but friends persuaded her to depart for the house of a friend in Virginia.

British troops set fire to the White House during their attack on Washington, DC, on August 24, 1814.

Shortly afterward, the president arrived back at the White House. Not finding Dolley there, he quickly left again. As he headed toward Virginia, Madison could see the buildings of Washington, DC, burning. That evening the British helped themselves to dinner in the White House kitchen and then set fire to the building.

★ CHAPTER FIVE ★

RESTORING PEACE

The day after the White House burned, Madison met with Dolley at a tavern near Great Falls, Virginia. From there he set off for Maryland to attempt to join Winder's troops and ended up spending the night in a postmaster's home, heavily guarded. On August 26, scouts reported that the British had left the capital. Madison feared that his fellow Americans would think their government had collapsed when the city burned, so he was eager to return as quickly as possible to show that the US government was still operational. Madison sent messages to his cabinet to join him and then headed back to the remains of the capital. With the White House uninhabitable, he moved into a residence on nearby F Street, where he had lived as Jefferson's secretary of state. Although he sent word to Dolley to stay where she was, she quickly joined him.

Meanwhile, Madison received messages from his military leaders, who had concerns about Armstrong. They blamed Armstrong's failure to act quickly for their inability to defend the capital. Many refused to take further orders from the secretary of war. The president did not agree with all the criticisms, but he knew Armstrong had failed to recognize the danger to the city and had not offered any ideas for protecting it. Madison spoke to

This painting shows the ruins of the US Capitol after British troops set fire to the building. Artist George Munger painted this watercolor in 1814.

Armstrong to suggest his resignation. Soon after their discussion, Armstrong resigned from the post. Madison put Monroe in charge of the War Department, in addition to the State Department, despite Monroe's previous reluctance to accept the role. In some historians' view, Madison should have taken action earlier to avoid such problems in his cabinet.

TURNING POINTS

The burning of Washington, DC, was a low point in the war for the Americans. However, soon after, the tide began to turn in their favor. In September 1814, American troops successfully fought off a British attack on Baltimore. The troops there were better prepared and better organized than the forces that had tried to defend the capital. British Major General Robert Ross was killed in the battle, a huge blow for Britain. That same month, the British also failed to take Fort McHenry, which was protecting Baltimore Harbor. Meanwhile, US troops defeated the

British at Lake Champlain, New York. It turned out to be a critical victory. About 10,000 British troops had been marching to New York, where they would face a force of a mere 3,400 US troops. It appeared to be a near certain victory for the British. But the British defeat at Lake Champlain put the British supply lines in danger. Not wanting to risk being cut off from supplies and reinforcements, the British withdrew into Canada.

With Washington, DC, in ruins, Congress argued about whether to move the capital to Philadelphia. Some thought it would be less expensive than rebuilding Washington and that the British would be unlikely to attack that far inland. Madison disagreed. He thought this would seem as if the government was fleeing. The House sided with Madison, voting against moving the capital city by 83 to 74.

The American and British fleets engaged in heavy gunfire on Lake Champlain near Plattsburgh, New York, on September 11, 1814.

FORT McHENRY

On September 13, 1814, the British tried to take Fort McHenry, which was protecting Baltimore's harbor. The attack lasted all day and night. But by the next morning, the American flag was still waving over the fort, signaling it had not fallen into British hands. American Francis Scott Key was aboard a British ship inquiring about the release of an American prisoner. He witnessed the battle and, that morning, wrote the words to a poem that eventually became "The Star-Spangled Banner." The song was later chosen as the United States' national anthem.

Francis Scott Key (center) was inspired to write what became the national anthem after watching the bombardment of Fort McHenry in 1814.

Meanwhile, the peace talks between the British and Americans continued in Ghent. When the president finally received word from his delegates, the news was disappointing. The British were demanding control of part of Maine and of the Great Lakes. Madison expected his negotiators to come home without an agreement, since the United States was not willing to yield on those issues.

AMERICANS DIVIDED

Madison had problems at home as well. In November 1814, more New England Federalists were elected to Congress. Some Federalist newspapers called for Madison to retire and turn over power to the Federalists. They blamed him for failing to protect the capital. Meanwhile, New Englanders unhappy with the war and trade restrictions called for change on a national scale. Massachusetts, Vermont, Rhode Island, New Hampshire, and Connecticut organized the Hartford Convention to discuss their mutual disagreements with Madison's administration. Madison feared the states would threaten to secede. Madison's vice president, Elbridge Gerry, urged him to write a persuasive manifesto on the importance of the Union.

Elbridge Gerry served as vice president from 1813 to 1814.

Others wanted the president to send in troops. Madison knew he must proceed with caution. "The course to be taken by the government is full of delicacy and perplexity," he wrote to a friend.

Thinking the best course of action was to gain a better understanding of the situation, Madison sent two military divisions, under the command of Colonel Thomas Jesup, into Connecticut. His official mission was to recruit more troops. But that was simply his cover. Madison had given Jesup secret orders to collect information on any talk of secession. In January, Madison's fears were calmed. The states were not yet planning to secede. But they did want a huge shift of power from the federal government to the New England states. The states wanted the power to control their own military and to manage the tax money that paid for it. If these demands were not granted, they planned to hold another convention, where the threat of secession might be on the table. Before they could present these demands to the president, however, the entire country's situation changed.

THE END OF THE WAR

In the fall of 1814, the British prepared a major attack on New Orleans, Louisiana, which provided access to both the Mississippi River and the Gulf of Mexico. Those who still opposed Madison thought a loss at New Orleans would prove them right about the president's leadership, especially since the country lacked the funds to continue fighting much longer. About fifty British warships carried seventy-five hundred British soldiers toward New Orleans. There, General Andrew Jackson led American troops in defense of their position. Under American artillery fire, the British had fallen back twice but each time regrouped to strike again. Finally, the British fled, with an estimated two thousand dead on their side, compared to just

General Andrew Jackson (on horseback) commands American troops to victory during the Battle of New Orleans on January 8, 1815.

thirteen Americans. On February 4, 1815, Madison received word of the results. Residents who had remained in Washington, DC, lit candles in celebration of what, at the moment, seemed like an important victory. When delegates from the Hartford Convention arrived in the capital on February 13 to air their grievances, their complaints were drowned out in the celebratory atmosphere.

Within days, the president received word from his delegates in Europe that they had agreed with the British on a peace treaty—the Treaty of Ghent. They had signed it two weeks before the Battle of New Orleans, but the news took time to reach North America. Congress approved the treaty on February 18. Speaking to Congress that day, Madison called peace a blessing. In the wake of secession talk, he urged lawmakers to continue to uphold the nation's laws and their states' loyalty to the Union. He also asked them to help build the nation's military

for the sake of the country's future security. The president expressed a hope that "the peace which has been just declared, will not only be the foundation of the most friendly intercourse between the United States and Great Britain, but that it will also be productive of happiness and harmony in every section of our beloved country."

Reaction to the Treaty of Ghent was split. On one hand, it did not give in to British demands for control of additional land or waters. But it also did not address impressment or any of Madison's original reasons for going to war. Critics have said this means the War of 1812 accomplished nothing, returning the situation to what it had been before the fighting began. Others have pointed out that because the world's circumstances had changed by the end of the war, Madison's original goals were

US and British representatives meet to sign the Treaty of Ghent on December 24, 1814. The treaty officially ended the War of 1812, but news of the peace agreement took time to reach the president and Congress.

irrelevant. By then Britain was no longer at war with France. Britain no longer had a reason to impress American sailors into its navy or to capture American ships. So the United States did not necessarily need the treaty to address those practices.

Aside from this, the war had shown the world that the United States would stand up for itself when other nations threatened its sovereignty. In November 1814, based on growing American military strength, the British government had directed its treaty negotiators to back off its demands. Despite their victories, the British noted that they had not made any progress in taking over US territory. The US Navy, in particular, earned the respect of the British. While tiny in comparison to Britain's, the US Navy had won approximately two-thirds of its fights at sea. US military

Throughout the war, the US Navy enjoyed considerable success against the much larger British Royal Navy.

power on land had gotten off to a much rockier start but had grown more organized and effective over time. One British writer noted that American soldiers were "increasing at every hour in skill, confidence, and numbers."

While the war undertaken by Madison had been controversial, many influential Americans agreed that it had been worthwhile. Former president John Adams said, "A more necessary war was never undertaken. It is necessary against England, necessary to convince France that we are something, and above all necessary to convince ourselves that we are not nothing."

★ CHAPTER SIX ★

DOMESTIC
POLICY

The issues of foreign policy and war dominated Madison's presidency, and they also drove much of his domestic policy. At the forefront was the question of funding the war effort—a constant struggle that forced Madison to revise many of his previous positions on the powers of the federal government. Chief among them was the existence of a national bank, an institution Madison had not supported during the early days of the Union.

THE NATIONAL BANK

The charter of the First Bank of the United States, approved by Congress in 1791, had expired in 1811, two years after Madison became president. Alexander Hamilton, Washington's secretary of the treasury, had originally devised the bank as a way for the country to pay off the debts incurred during the American Revolution. It also enabled the creation of a stable, consistent national currency to replace the many different bills and coins issued by states prior to its existence.

Madison vehemently opposed the institution during Washington's presidency. He did not think that Article 1, Section 8 of the Constitution, which gave Congress the power to provide for the country's general welfare and pass laws deemed "necessary and proper," permitted the government to establish a bank. He feared that such a broad reading of the Constitution would give the federal government unlimited power on numerous issues that the founders had intended to leave under the states' control. Madison had many conversations with Washington trying to persuade him to veto the bill, but the president signed it.

By the time the bank's charter was set to expire twenty years later, it had become a crucial part of the nation's finances. In 1811, as war with Britain drew closer, Madison knew that the country would need a source of loans. His reluctance to let

Congress approved a charter for the First Bank of the United States in 1791. Although he opposed the charter at the time, Madison later came to see the bank as a necessary part of the US economy and supported it.

NECESSARY AND PROPER

During Madison's presidency, much disagreement centered on the interpretation of a clause in the Constitution that gives Congress authority to make any law that is *necessary and proper* to carry out the powers and duties laid out for it in the Constitution. Those who favor a strict construction of the Constitution, such as Madison, argue that the word *necessary* is restrictive. It limits what Congress can do. In 1819, after Madison's presidency, US Supreme Court Chief Justice John Marshall interpreted the word *necessary* to mean anything that is useful to accomplish an end. This clause is often called the elastic clause because it gives the government the ability to expand and adapt as the country's needs change over time.

the federal government grow too powerful had to be balanced with the practical needs of funding an adequate military. So he was resigned to renewing the bank's charter for this purpose. However, he faced an uphill battle in convincing his own administration and members of his party in Congress, who were also devoted to limiting the scope of the federal government. Secretary of the Treasury Albert Gallatin worked on Madison's behalf to promote the charter's renewal, but Gallatin was unpopular in the Senate. Meanwhile, secretary of state Robert Smith was working to undermine Gallatin's efforts in the Senate. When the issue came to a vote, it was a tie. Madison's vice president, George Clinton, cast the deciding vote. Still bitter that he had not been nominated to run for president, Clinton voted against it, and the charter was not renewed.

With no national bank in place, the federal government lost its ability to issue public banknotes to fund debt. It would have to depend on private loans and taxes to pay and equip its military. Congress agreed to borrow $11 million to fund the effort. But the issue of taxes was almost as controversial among Republicans as the bank had been. Madison directed Gallatin to ask Congress

Albert Gallatin served as secretary of the treasury for two presidents— Thomas Jefferson and James Madison.

to reinstate taxes on imports and taxes on property within the United States. These were the very taxes that had contributed to the Federalists' fall from power just a decade earlier. Some Republicans feared they too would suffer political consequences if they supported these taxes. Others found themselves in a position similar to the president's, reluctantly facing the reality of funding the war. After vigorous debate, Congress agreed to pass the taxes, but said that they would only be levied if and when war was declared.

Once the conflict began, the country still struggled to fund its military. Opponents of the war saw an opportunity to starve the war effort by persuading private banks not to loan money to the US government. Public funds dried up, and the country could not pay its debts or its soldiers. On September 20, 1814, the president addressed Congress in the patent office, one of the few remaining public buildings still standing in Washington, DC. Madison asked for more taxes to further fund the war, but Congress failed to provide more funds. Even when the Treasury became unable to pay the interest on its existing loans, no new taxes were levied. The government defaulted on its loans for several months by not making payments on the interest it owed.

In 1815, riding high on a surge of popularity following the war's end, Madison once again said the United States needed a national bank. By then Madison had seen firsthand why the country needed a reliable source of funds. He justified his change of position by stating that he was following "legislative precedent." Madison argued that the government should follow the examples set by previous legislative bodies.

SEPARATING CHURCH AND STATE

As president, Madison maintained his philosophy of religious freedom. In 1811 he vetoed a bill that would have founded a government-sanctioned church in Washington, DC, and another bill that would have given public land to a church in Mississippi. When Congress urged him to issue a proclamation calling for a wartime day of prayer, Madison said that people could pray if they wanted to pray. (He later relented, but his position was clear.) He received critical letters from citizens who wanted him to do more to promote Christianity. But Madison maintained that church and state must remain separate.

Finally, Congress was convinced, and Madison signed a law re-creating the national bank in April 1816. He also persuaded Congress to pass a law establishing a regular military staff and strengthening the navy. This was another issue on which Madison had changed his position. Earlier in his career, he had thought that a strong military would make the federal government too powerful, at the expense of the rights of its people. But years of war had convinced him that this was necessary for national security.

EXPANSION INTO AMERICAN INDIAN TERRITORY

During Madison's presidency, the United States continued to expand its territories. American expansion came at the expense of American Indians who had occupied the lands long before the arrival of Europeans. As more Europeans moved west, many American Indians fought to retain their lands. In the territory of Indiana, Governor William Henry Harrison had negotiated a series of eight treaties with the Shawnee during Jefferson's presidency. But by the time Madison was president, two Shawnee brothers, Tenskwatawa (called the Prophet) and Tecumseh,

Shawnee spiritual leader Tenskwatawa urged American Indian groups to resist Europeans attempting to settle on their lands.

Shawnee leader Tecumseh (center) confronts Governor William Henry Harrison (right) in Vincennes, Indiana, in August 1810. Harrison negotiated treaties with American Indian groups during Thomas Jefferson's presidency.

had united the Shawnee peoples in resistance. They were unwilling to give up any more of their land.

Madison's secretary of war, William Eustis, sent troops to Indiana to help Harrison. Harrison was told to use the troops only as defense and not to attack the Shawnee. So Harrison took action to provoke a Shawnee attack. He marched the troops to camp near the Shawnee settlement of Prophetstown on the Tippecanoe and Wabash Rivers. Harrison did not post lookouts, intentionally leaving the camp vulnerable to attack. The Shawnee took the bait, and a battle broke out. After suffering many American casualties, Harrison took over Prophetstown and declared victory.

Although Harrison had deliberately caused the conflict, many governors and other politicians grew uneasy about the possibility

of American Indian raids. Madison issued a proclamation on December 18, 1811, assuring the country that Harrison's victory at Tippecanoe would lead to peace on the western frontier. The following spring, the president used the collective fear that the British were encouraging American Indian raids to build support for the coming war.

Some American Indian peoples, particularly the Shawnee, had hoped the War of 1812 would help them hold onto their lands. But after Tecumseh was defeated at the Battle of the Thames, Shawnee resistance crumbled. The United States gained tighter control of the Northwest Territory, and more Americans of European descent moved into the area.

American Indian warriors fight Harrison and his troops during the Battle of Tippecanoe on November 7, 1811. After the battle, Harrison and his men burned Prophetstown, while Tenskwatawa and the Shawnee people traveled north to ally with British forces.

WEST FLORIDA

When Madison had helped Jefferson negotiate for the Louisiana Purchase in 1803, both believed that land in West Florida, which included an area between the Mississippi and Perdido Rivers, had been included in the deal. However, France disagreed and turned the land over to Spain in 1804. In September 1810, a group of Americans acting on their own decided to seize control of the land and then offer it to the United States. The following month, Madison issued the proclamation asserting that the United States had maintained the rights to the land since 1803. He directed William C. C. Claiborne, governor of the nearby Territory of Orleans, to make sure the land stayed under US control. Congress approved these actions in January 1811.

Jefferson (seated) approved the Louisana Purchase in 1803. The agreement expanded US territories, but border disagreements continued into Madison's presidency.

The Creek Indians of the Southeast also had been British allies during the War of 1812. Inspired by Tecumseh and angered by the encroachment on their land, a group of Creek allies known as the Red Sticks attacked white settlements in Alabama and Georgia in 1813. Southerners responded with an army of five thousand militiamen, led by General Andrew Jackson. By the fall of 1813, Jackson had wiped out the Creek settlements of Tallasahatchee and Talladega. At the Battle of Horseshoe Bend on March 27, 1814, about three thousand militiamen faced one thousand Creek warriors. The Americans killed more than eight hundred of the Creek men and captured five hundred Creek women and children. In a treaty signed on August 9, the Creek agreed to turn over 23 million acres (9.3 million hectares) of land—roughly half of Georgia and part of southern Alabama—to the US government. Madison rewarded Jackson for these victories by promoting him to the rank of brigadier general.

★ CHAPTER SEVEN ★

MADISON'S FINAL YEARS

With the war widely considered a success, Madison's popularity rebounded in his final two years in office. Many Americans felt a renewed sense of pride in and loyalty to their country. The Federalists lost popularity and soon dropped out of power. John Adams, the nation's second president, wrote of Madison's presidency, "Notwithstanding a thousand Faults and blunders [Madison] has acquired more glory, and established more union; than all his three predecessors . . . put together."

As free trade resumed and local economies started to recover, even New Englanders expressed support for the president. Madison received a letter from Boston residents apologizing for their previous discontent and praising the president for "defending our commercial rights from foreign Aggressions & maintaining the honor of the American Flag against those who had arrogantly assumed the Sovereignty of the Ocean."

The restored trade—and the import taxes that came with it—also helped the national treasury to recover after the war. And rebuilding in Washington, DC, began shortly after the war. Madison directed architect Benjamin Latrobe to restore the White

Architect Benjamin Latrobe was given the task of rebuilding the Capitol and the White House after their destruction during the war. He drew this illustration of the new White House in 1817.

House as closely to its original structure as possible, and the new building was completed in 1817.

After the approval of the national bank, the president did not take an active policy role for the remainder of his second term, but he did speak up on one issue close to his heart. In his 1815 message for Congress, he asked for a federally funded university to be located in Washington, DC. While normally Madison objected to the federal government establishing institutions not mentioned in the Constitution, he felt that higher learning served a national interest of promoting liberty instead of limiting it. He urged Congress to support "the advancement of knowledge, without which the blessings of liberty cannot be fully enjoyed or long preserved." However, Congress took no action on this request. Exhausted by the war and experiencing recurring health problems, Madison returned to Montpelier in the spring of 1816.

CONSTITUTIONAL LEGACY

In his last address to Congress in December 1816, shortly before he turned over the presidency to Monroe, Madison expressed pride that the country had reached forty years of independence. He thanked Americans for upholding the Constitution for those four decades, even in trying times.

Historians have praised Madison for respecting the Constitution even when the country was at war and factions within the United States were in conflict. Many believe one of Madison's most significant achievements was proving that a country could be both powerful and democratic at the same time. In particular, Madison had chosen to uphold the First Amendment instead of attempting to silence his many critics. James Blake, then mayor of Washington, DC, spoke on this matter several days before Madison left office. Nations rarely achieve power and glory without sacrificing personal liberty, Blake said. He praised Madison for guiding the country through war without infringing on individuals' rights. All the while, Madison had continued his fight for religious freedom and the separation of church and state.

Madison delivered this farewell address to Congress on December 3, 1816. In his speech, Madison thanked Americans for upholding the Constitution.

In one of his last acts of office, Madison upheld his interpretation of the Constitution once again. Earlier he had spoken about the need to improve the country's roads and canals, but he believed a constitutional amendment would be needed to give Congress the power to act. Congress passed a national improvements bill, known as the Bonus Bill, without amending the Constitution first.

Gilbert Stuart painted this portrait of Madison in 1821.

Madison maintained his position that the federal government only possessed powers specifically outlined in the Constitution. He argued that this expenditure of federal money could not be construed as necessary or proper, as required by a strict interpretation of the Constitution. On these grounds, Madison vetoed the Bonus Bill on his last day in office. Ignoring the limits set by the Constitution, as he had argued before, meant "the parchment had better be thrown into the fire at once."

Madison continued to argue for a stricter interpretation of the Constitution after his presidency. In the 1819 Supreme Court decision *McCulloch v. Maryland*, Chief Justice John Marshall declared that, in addition to the powers specifically listed in the Constitution, Congress also possessed whatever powers it needed to carry out its constitutional duties. These powers were known as implied powers. The case dealt with the creation of a national bank, which Madison had favored late in his presidency. But Madison did not agree with the broadness of the court's interpretation. Madison wrote to a Virginia appeals court judge explaining his opinion. According to Madison, the framers did not intend to give Congress such broad authority. He also did not think that the states would have ratified the Constitution if they

In 1819 Chief Justice John Marshall argued that Congress possessed powers beyond those outlined in the Constitution.

believed it would make the federal government so powerful. The issue continued to be debated for decades after *McCulloch v. Maryland*. Over time, most of the country adopted Marshall's broader interpretation.

Although Madison thought the federal government should be limited in power, he believed it should hold authority over the states. In 1832 South Carolina attempted to challenge federal authority by declaring a federal tariff null and void within the state. This came to be known as the nullification crisis. President Andrew Jackson issued a federal proclamation asserting federal authority over states, and Madison wrote several papers in support of Jackson's position.

VIEWS ON SLAVERY

While Madison did not take any action on the issue of slavery while in office, he gave much thought to the moral and practical issues surrounding slavery once he returned to Montpelier. As a

large plantation owner, Madison owned about one hundred slaves, but his commitment to personal liberties made the issue of slavery difficult for him. He wrote in 1825, "The magnitude of this evil among us is so deeply felt, and so universally acknowledged, that no merit could be greater than that of devising a satisfactory remedy for it." But he wrestled with the logistics of emancipation, especially the question of how plantation owners—himself included—would cope without slave labor. He continued to own slaves for the rest of his life because he did not think his plantation could afford to operate without slave labor, and he worried about Dolley's financial security following his death.

The country began to debate the issue of slavery fervently when Congress approved the Missouri Compromise in 1821. Missouri had first attempted to become a state in 1817, but legislators could not agree on whether slavery would be restricted in a new state. The Missouri Compromise admitted

The Montpelier estate covers over 2,000 acres (809 hectares) in Virginia. The Madison family owned one hundred slaves to work in the house and fields of the large plantation.

AGRICULTURAL INNOVATIONS

After he left office and returned to Montpelier, Madison became president of the Agricultural Society of Albemarle. As the organization's leader, he advocated for farming methods that would preserve the land. He spoke to members about the importance of not planting the same crop on the same land year after year, a practice that drains the soil of its nutrients. He also supported the use of fertilizer, plowing methods that kept seeds from washing away in the rain, and irrigation to bring water to dry land. Additionally, Madison spoke out about the importance of preserving trees. Many forests had already been cut down by that time to make way for farmland.

Missouri into the union with no restrictions on slavery there but banned slavery in western states north of Missouri's southern border. The agreement split the country into free states and slave states. Madison worried that the country's division on the issue of slavery would lead to future conflicts. Furthermore, he knew that the end of slavery would mean the end of Southern agricultural practices that depended on slave labor.

To express these fears, Madison wrote an allegory featuring a husband and a wife, symbolizing the North and the South. Before marriage, the husband and wife both had black stains on their arms, but the husband was able to remove his easily. After they were wed, he told his wife to get rid of the black stain on her arm too, even though removing the stain in her case would be more difficult. It would mean cutting off her arm and bleeding to death. The black stain represented slavery. Madison

was expressing his opinion that slavery was a necessary evil. He thought that forcing the South to end slavery would destroy the economies of many states.

Madison did hope the country could gradually free its slaves. He supported transporting freed slaves to Africa where they would escape white prejudice. "To be consistent with existing and probably unalterable prejudices in the US, the freed blacks ought to be permanently removed beyond the region occupied by or allotted to a white population," Madison wrote. Madison was a key member of the American Colonization Society, which supported this plan. Members of the society raised money to free slaves and then transport them to Liberia in Africa. At first the society was controversial because it opposed slavery. Later it drew criticism from abolitionists, including many free African Americans, who opposed ridding the United States of its free black population.

Madison received this membership certificate from the American Colonization Society in 1816. The society favored transporting freed slaves from the United States to settlements in Liberia.

THE LAST FOUNDER

Eighty-five-year-old James Madison died on June 28, 1836, six days before the country's sixtieth birthday. While he has been revered as the Father of the Constitution and champion of the Bill of Rights, few historians have ranked him among the nation's greatest presidents. The circumstances of war against Great Britain consumed most of the years he was in office, preventing him from having an impact on a wider range of other issues. And many have faulted him for his handling of the war, for pursuing strategies that ended in failure, and for filling his cabinet with questionable choices. Yet Madison's style of leadership made him enormously popular in his final years in office. And while his strict interpretation of the Constitution has mostly fallen out of favor, his vision of a strong central government that trumped the states has lasted. Madison's views on many questions evolved as he faced the reality of governing. He has been praised for both his willingness to reconsider his views on some issues as the nation's circumstances changed and for his steadfast adherence to those he held dearest—the constitutional liberties he campaigned for early in his career.

Asher Brown Durand painted this portrait of an elderly Madison in 1833.

UNIVERSITY OF VIRGINIA

Madison believed that education and the free flow of knowledge and ideas were essential to a democratic society. "A popular Government, without popular information, or the means of acquiring it, is but a Prologue to a Farce or a Tragedy; or, perhaps both," he wrote to a friend in 1822. "Knowledge will forever govern ignorance: And a people who mean to be their own Governors, must arm themselves with the power which knowledge gives." Because he felt education was so important, Madison helped Jefferson found the University of Virginia. The school opened in 1825. Madison served on the board and took over as head of the university in 1826, following Jefferson's death.

James Madison helped Thomas Jefferson to found the University of Virginia in Charlottesville, Virginia. In modern times, the university enrolls about twenty thousand students.

By the end of his presidency, Madison had achieved his most important goal: ensuring that the country he had helped to create survived the threat to its independence and unity. Near the end of his life, he wrote a note titled "Advice to my Country," which was opened after his death. "The advice nearest to my heart and deepest in my convictions," he had written, "is that the Union of the States be cherished and perpetuated."

TIMELINE

1751   James Madison is born in Port Conway, Virginia, to James Madison and Nelly Conway Madison.

1787   Madison presents the Virginia Plan, supporting a strong national government, at the Constitutional Convention in Philadelphia, Pennsylvania.

1789   Madison is elected to the US House of Representatives, where he pushes for the passage of the Bill of Rights.

1792   Madison joins with Thomas Jefferson to found the Republican Party.

1801   Madison becomes Jefferson's secretary of state.

1807   Madison persuades Jefferson to support the Embargo Act, ending all foreign trade.

1808   Madison is elected fourth president of the United States.

1809   Just before Madison takes office, the unsuccessful Embargo Act is repealed.

1812   Unable to stop the British policy of impressment through trade sanctions, Madison asks Congress to declare war on Great Britain. Madison is reelected to a second term.

1814   British forces invade Washington, DC, and set fire to the White House.

1815   General Andrew Jackson defeats the British at New Orleans, before receiving word that the Treaty of Ghent had been signed, ending the war.

1816   Madison signs a law to establish a national bank in the United States.

1817   Madison leaves office shortly after vetoing a bill that would have provided federal funding to build roads and canals, citing a lack of constitutional authority.

        After leaving office, Madison joins with Jefferson and others to help found the University of Virginia.

1836   On June 28, Madison dies at the age of eighty-five.

SOURCE NOTES

6   Lynne Cheney, *James Madison: A Life Reconsidered* (New York: Penguin, 2014), 265.

6   Ibid., 266.

8   Ibid.

12   Ibid., 25.

12   Ibid., 28.

13   Garry Wills, *James Madison* (New York: Times, 2002), 17.

15–16   Cheney, *James Madison*, 57.

16   Ibid.

17   Ralph Ketcham, *James Madison: A Biography* (Charlottesville: University of Virginia Press, 1990), 201.

19   Cheney, *James Madison*, 88.

21   Ibid., 101.

21   "Colleagues and Friends: James Monroe," James Madison's Montpelier, accessed June 22, 2015, http://www.montpelier.org/james-and-dolley-madison/james-madison/politician-and-statesman/colleagues/james-monroe.

22   Ibid., 144.

23   Ibid., 147.

24   "James Madison," *Encyclopædia Britannica*, last modified July 31, 2014, http://www.britannica.com/EBchecked/topic/355859/James-Madison.

25   Cheney, *James Madison*, 155.

25   Ibid.

27   Hugh Howard, *Mr. and Mrs. Madison's War: America's First Couple and the War of 1812* (New York: Bloomsbury Press, 2012), 53.

28   Cheney, *James Madison*, 220.

29   Wills, *James Madison*, 62–63.

31   Cheney, *James Madison*, 213.

38–39   Wills, *James Madison*, 92.

51   Cheney, *James Madison*, 243.

53   Ibid., 244–245.

55   Ibid., 247.

58   Ibid., 251.

60   Ibid., 265.

60   Howard, *Mr. and Mrs. Madison's War*, 135.

67   Cheney, *James Madison*, 259.

69   "Special Message from Congress on the Treaty of Ghent," Miller Center, University of Virginia, accessed June 1, 2015, http://millercenter.org/president/madison/speeches/speech-3627.

71   Cheney, *James Madison*, 262.

71   Ibid., 263.

76   Ibid., 264.

82   Robert Allen Rutland, *James Madison: The Founding Father* (New York: MacMillan, 1987), 237.

82   Ibid., 232.

83   Ibid., 236.

85   Cheney, *James Madison*, 266.

87   James Madison, ed. Ralph Ketcham, *Selected Writings of James Madison* (Indianapolis: Hackett, 2006), 322.

89 Madison, *Selected Writings*, 315.

91 "Page 1 of James Madison to W. T. Barry, August 4, 1822," Library of Congress, accessed June 4, 2015, http://www.loc.gov/resource /mjm.20_0155_0159/?sp=1&st=text.

92 Frank Freidel and Hugh Sidey, "James Madison," *The Presidents of the United States*, online at *WhiteHouse.gov*, accessed June 1, 2015, https://www.whitehouse.gov/1600/presidents/jamesmadison.

GLOSSARY

allegory: a story in which characters and events are symbols that stand for larger ideas

bicameral: having two parts

blockade: an act of war in which one country uses ships to stop people or supplies from entering or leaving another country

boycott: to refuse to buy goods or services as a form of protest

colony: an area controlled by a country that is usually far away from it

confederacy: a group of people, countries, or states that have joined together for some purpose

delegate: a person chosen to act or vote for others

embargo: a government order that limits trade

Federalist: someone who supports a strong central government

frigate: a small and fast military ship

impressment: the act of seizing something for public use

nullification: action by a state to impede or prevent the enforcement of a US law

precedent: an earlier action or decision that sets an example to justify what follows

proportional: having a size or number directly related to the size of something else

ratify: to make a treaty, amendment, or other official document official by signing or voting for it

sovereignty: a country's independent authority and right to govern itself

SELECTED BIBLIOGRAPHY

"American President: James Madison (1751–1836)." Miller Center, University of Virginia. Accessed June 15, 2014. http://millercenter.org/president/madison/essays/biography/1.

Burstein, Andrew, and Nancy Isenberg. *Madison and Jefferson.* New York: Random House, 2010.

Cheney, Lynne. *James Madison: A Life Reconsidered.* New York: Penguin, 2014.

Freidel, Frank, and Hugh Sidey. "James Madison." In *The Presidents of the United States of America.* WhiteHouse.gov. Accessed June 1, 2015. https://www.whitehouse.gov/1600/presidents/jamesmadison.

"James Madison." *Encyclopædia Britannica.* Last modified July 31, 2014. http://www.britannica.com/EBchecked/topic/355859/James-Madison.

"The James Madison Papers, 1723–1836." Library of Congress. Accessed June 4, 2015. http://www.loc.gov/collections/james-madison-papers/about-this-collection/.

Ketcham, Ralph. *James Madison: A Biography.* Charlottesville: University of Virginia Press, 1990.

Labunski, Richard. *James Madison and the Struggle for the Bill of Rights.* New York: Oxford University Press, 2006.

Rutland, Robert Allen. *James Madison: The Founding Father.* New York: MacMillan, 1987.

Wills, Garry. *James Madison.* New York: Times, 2002.

FURTHER INFORMATION

American Presidents Life Portraits: James Madison
http://www.americanpresidents.org/presidents/president.
asp?PresidentNumber=4
This website, created as a companion to a series by C-SPAN, profiles US presidents.

Goddu, Krystyna Poray. *George Washington's Presidency*. Minneapolis: Lerner Publications, 2016. Go behind the scenes of the administration of the nation's first president, see the role James Madison played in politics at the time, and learn more about political developments that laid the groundwork for events in Madison's presidency.

Greenblatt, Miriam. *The War of 1812*. New York: Chelsea House, 2010. Learn more about the political climate and trade issues that led to the War of 1812, as well as the details of how the war was fought.

History: James Madison
http://www.history.com/topics/us-presidents/james-madison
Access articles, videos, and speeches related to the fourth US president.

Larson, Edward J., and Michael P. Winship. *The Constitutional Convention: A Narrative History from the Notes of James Madison*. New York: Modern Library, 2005. This collection of Madison's notes on the Constitutional Convention provides an inside look at the decisions that went into the making of this important document.

The Library of Congress: The Federalist Papers
http://thomas.loc.gov/home/histdox/fedpapers.html
Find the complete *Federalist Papers*, written by James Madison, Alexander Hamilton, and John Jay.

Marsico, Katie. *The War of 1812*. Edina, MN: Abdo, 2011.
Find out more about what the United States was fighting for in the War of 1812 and how the young nation survived the conflict.

Profiles of US Presidents: James Madison
http://www.presidentprofiles.com/Washington-Johnson/Madison
-James.html
Visit this site for a detailed exploration of Madison's early years, presidency, and later years, plus an extensive bibliography.

Sharp, Constance. *Thomas Jefferson and the Growing United States (1800–1811)*. Philadelphia: Mason Crest Publishers, 2012. Investigate the presidency and policies of Thomas Jefferson, James Madison's closest political ally.

VanDuren, Mau. *Many Heads and Many Hands: James Madison's Search for a More Perfect Union*. Franktown, VA: Northampton House, 2015. VanDuren offers readers a glimpse of Madison's vision of the Constitution and his continuing efforts to uphold it.

White House: James Madison
https://www.whitehouse.gov/1600/presidents/jamesmadison
Read the White House's official biography of the nation's fourth president.

INDEX

PHOTO ACKNOWLEDGMENTS

The images in this book are used with the permission of: © iStockphoto.com/hudiemm (sunburst); © iStockphoto.com/Nic_Taylor (parchment); © iStockphoto.com/Phil Cardamone (bunting); Document courtesy of the James Madison Papers at the Library of Congress, p. 2 (background); © Universal History Archive/Getty Images, p. 2 (portrait); Signature courtesy of the James Madison Papers at the Library of Congress, p. 3; © Everett Collection Historical/Alamy, p. 7; © Andia/Alamy, p. 9; © De Agostini Picture Library/Bridgeman Images, pp. 11, 69; © North Wind Picture Archives/Alamy, pp. 13, 31, 61; Library of Congress, pp. 14, 26, 41, 50, 55, 58, 59 (left), 63, 65, 66, 68, 79, 83, 89; National Archives, pp. 16, 18, 46, 53; © ClassicStock/Alamy, p. 19; © New York Public Library/Bridgeman Images, p. 20; © CORBIS, pp. 23, 80; © Collection of the New York Historical Society/Bridgeman Images, pp. 25, 49, 90; © Musee de la Marine /Bridgeman Images, p. 29; © Peter Newark Pictures/Bridgeman Images, pp. 30, 35, 44, 45, 51, 77; The Granger Collection, New York, pp. 33, 84; Courtesy of Naval History and Heritage Command, Photo Archives, p. 34; © B Christopher/Alamy, p. 36; © The Trustees of the British Museum/Art Resource, NY, p. 38; © MixPix/Alamy, p. 43; © Stock Montage, Inc./Alamy, p. 54; © Laura Westlund/Independent Picture Service, p. 56; © Brooklyn Museum of Art/Bridgeman Images, p. 59 (right); © Christie's Images/ Bridgeman Images, p. 64; © Thomas Birch/SuperStock/Getty Images, p. 70; © MPI/Getty Images, p. 73; © nsf/Alamy, p. 75; © Kean Collection/Getty Images, p. 78; © Mead Art Museum, Amherst College, MA/Bridgeman Images, p. 85; © Boltin Picture Library/Bridgeman Images, p. 86; © Mark Summerfield/Alamy, p. 87; © Philip Scalia/Alamy, p. 91.

Front cover: Document courtesy of the James Madison Papers at the Library of Congress; Portrait of James Madison by John Vanderlyn, courtesy of White House Historical Association/Wikimedia Commons/ (PD); Signature courtesy of the James Madison Papers at the Library of Congress;© iStockphoto.com/WilshireImages (flag bunting).

Back cover: © iStockphoto.com/hudiemm (sunburst); © iStockphoto.com/ Nic_Taylor (parchment).

ABOUT THE AUTHOR

Erika Wittekind is a book editor and the author of nearly a dozen nonfiction books for children and young adults. A former newspaper reporter, Wittekind earned degrees in journalism and political science at Bradley University. She lives in Wisconsin.